SHIFTING PRESPECTIVES
PART ONE . LOST VOICES
Makayla Crain

Copyright © 2025 Makayla Crain

All rights reserved.

ISBN-13:979-8-3070-4835-1

DEDICATION

Amidst all the bickering and little sisterly squabbles,
My love for you all runs deeper than words can express.
As I write this heartfelt message, I find myself moved to tears, for you all are uniquely beautiful. This dedication is a reminder that anything is achievable, regardless of our ages. I want you to know that I am always here for you: Sarah, Mya, Jakayla.
Mom, no matter what path I chose, you supported me. Your unwavering support has meant to the world to me. I can never fully convey how grateful I am for you.

CONTENTS

	Acknowledgments	i
1	Growing Up	Pg #1
2	A Love story in two seasons	Pg #2
3	Bridges Made of Words	Pg #3
4	The Weight of Hope	Pg #4
5	Dance of Change	Pg #5
6	Beyond Labels	Pg #6
7	Soul's Reflection	Pg #7
8	Seeking	Pg #8
9	The Mind's Maze	Pg #9
10	The Puzzle of Real	Pg #10
11	The Empty Canvas	Pg# 11
12	The River of Time	Pg# 12
13	Life's Journey	Pg#13
14	The Tide of Grief	Pg#14
15	Greif's Journey	Pg#16
16	Dreams Fade	Pg# 17
17	The Pull	Pg#18
18	The Ever-Changing Me	Pg#19

19	The Many Faces of War	Pg#20
20	Four Sides of the Coin	Pg#21
21	Warming World	Pg#22
22	The Gap	Pg#23
23	Wires and Waves	Pg#24
24	The Wheel of Time	Pg#25
25	The Shadow's Dance	Pg#26
26	The Cage of Choice	Pg#27
27	The Brush of Truth	Pg#28
28	The Clock Tick-Tocks	Pg#29
29	Pathway	Pg#30
30	Dreams Evolves	Pg#31
31	Evolving Faith	Pg#32
32	The Web of Life	Pg#33
33	The Evolving Self	Pg#34
34	Grateful Heart	Pg#35
35	The Seeds of Change	Pg#36
36	Faces of War	Pg#37

37	The Immigrant's Journey	Pg#38
38	A Just and Equal World	Pg#39
39	Digital Natives	Pg# 40
40	The Long Goodbye	Pg#41
41	Sunset's Peace	Pg#42
42	Painted Perfection	Pg#43
43	Real Beauty	Pg#44
44	Shadows and light	Pg#45
45	Twisted Tales	Pg#46
46	The Boil	Pg#47
47	Miror, Mirror	Pg#48
48	Bottled Up	Pg#49
49	The Grudge	Pg#50
50	Shadows Within	Pg#51
51	Simmering	Pg#52
52	The Art of Forgiveness	Pg#53
53	The Sting	Pg#54

54 Red   Pg#55

55 Silent Walls Pg#56

56 Words That Wound Pg#57

57 Empty Words   Pg#58

58 Walls   Pg# 59

59 Words like Daggers Pg# 60

60 Sticks and Stones Pg# 61

61 Quite Fury   Pg# 62

62 Broken Pieces Pg# 63

63 Enough is Enough Pg# 64

64 Heavy Chains Pg# 65

65 Turning Away Pg#66

66 Simple Joys Pg# 67

67 Warm Embrace Pg#68

68 Little Eyes   Pg#69

68 Small Joys   Pg#70

69 Heart's Dance Pg# 71

70 Two Hearts as One Pg#72

71 Happy Times Pg#73

72 Warm Hug Pg# 74

73 Friends Together Pg#75

74 Giving Gift Pg#76

75 New Day's Song Pg# 77

76 Starry Sky Pg#78

77 Life's Gentle Flow Pg#79

78 Creative Spark Pg#80

79 Tiny Lights Pg# 81

80 Surprise of Joy Pg#82

81 Why? Pg# 83

82 What Is It Worth Pg# 84

ACKNOWLEDGMENTS

These remarkable women played a significant role in the creation of this book, and I am sincerely grateful to Jessica McGee and Diana Townsend.

Growing Up

I'm grown, they say, with a pat on the back,

"Yes ma'am, no ma'am, yes sir, no sir," it's the adult track.

But why can't we as kids get the same respect, told to stay in our place, like we're not correct?

We may be young, but we've got a voice, we've got dreams and ideas, we've got our own choice.

We're not just children, we're future leaders in the making, we deserve to be seen, not dismissed for the taking.

We may be small, but our dreams are big and bright,

You tell us to mind our Ps and Qs and dim our light.

You try to keep us quiet, out of sight,

But we'll ignite and burn so bright.

A LOVE STORY IN TWO SEASONS

In springtime's warm glow,

Hearts like blossoms in the sun,
Love's river starts to flow,
Paths of two becoming one.

Moonlight cast a spell,
Whispers soft as night unfolds,
Charmed by secrets only we tell,
New love,
A story untold.

But shadows start to creep,
Roses wither,
Petals fall,
Promises we failed to keep,
Walls rise where hearts once stood tall.

Now winter chills the air,
Frozen whispers
Silent cries,
Love's journey laid bare
Beneath disillusioned skies.

Bridges Made of Words

In the quiet daybreak,

Your voice is a lighthouse,

guiding me through the fog,

each syllable a ship,

sailing across the vast ocean of longing.

We build our castle in the air,

Brick by brick-hope in one hand,

Disappointment in the other,

The irony of love stretching like elastic;

It bends but never breaks.

The Weight of Hope

In fields once kissed by sunlight's grace,
A childhood dance, dreams embraced,
Yet shadows loom where cannons roar,
And innocence begins to soar.

Through shattered streets and renting skies,
A journey forged in silent cries,
With every step, a heavy cost-
The ghosts of the home are forever lost.

But through the tears and fear's grim tale,
In foreign lands, they still set sail;
For deep within, ambition burns,
A quest for justice, hope returns.

Dance of Change

Oh, dear friend, as seasons sway and spin,
The scientists murmur facts, where to begin?
While politicians' debate in halls polished bright,
Activists rally; their dreams are taking flight.

Yet shadows linger where oceans now rise, Nature signs softly, but beauty still lies.

Amidst the conflict of humanity's plight,
Justice whispers gently in the soft, golden light.

Beyond Labels

In a world that wants to define me
By the color of my skin they see,
I refuse to be boxed in, confined,
I am more than just a simple line.

I am Black, yes, it's true,
But my Hispanic heritage shines through,
I will not let anyone dictate
The pride I have in my mixed state.

I am a blend of two worlds, both strong,
A fusion of cultures where I belong,
I will not let anyone put me down,
With their narrow views and judgements brown.

I am Black, I am Hispanic, I am proud,
I will not let others silence me with a shroud,
I will break free from this cage they've built,
And stand tall with the strength I have built.

I will embrace every part of me,
My roots, my history, my identity,
I am Black, I am Hispanic, I am a Boricua
And that is all I'll ever need.

Soul's ~~Reflection~~

In the echoing halls where shadows play,
A youth 's heart thunders,
Beating loud and clear.

With every step,
The whispers sway,
A journey begun,
Shedding masks of fear.

Through storms of doubt,
 The wind whooshes past,
Eyes like mirrors seeking the core inside.

Finding oneself in reflections cast,
Against the tide's roar,
 a soul defied.

The clanging clash of dreams unmet,
Shapes a spirit bold,
Yet tender still.

In silence deep as night's silhouette,
Emerge strength forged by sheer will.

With each tik-tock of time's grand clock,
The path revealed bright clarity.

Embracing now the thunderous shock,
Of finding truth in identity.

Seeking

Paths diverge in thought,
Echoes of youth linger near-
What did I become?

Dreams once bright as stars,
Fading into whispers now,
What must I pursue?

Mirrors hold my gaze,
Reflections twist and expand-
Which way leads me home?

Years like flowing streams,
Craving doubts in silent stone,
Still, I seek the light.

Future calls my name,
With each step, the heart races-
Can I find my way?

Through the thorns of time,
Questions bloom like wildflowers-
Life's meaning unfolds.

The Mind's Maze

The world spins, a blur,
Colors mix, a messy stir.
Thoughts race, a wild, fast flow,
Whispers creep, soft and low.

Logic fades, a distant shore,
Shadows loom, forevermore.
A calmer mind, a peaceful kind.
But voices rise, sharp, and mean,
"You're weak, you're lost, a broken scene."

The mirror shows a stranger's face,
Lost in the maze, without a trace.
A flicker bright, of hope's small spark,
To pierce the dark, a guiding mark.

A longing deep, for things to be,
Normal and clear, for you and me.

The Puzzle of Real

Is it all just a dream, a mind's design?
Or atoms dancing, a grand machine?
Do we make meaning, or is it all there,
A waiting truth, beyond compare.

Idealism whispers, a mind's embrace,
The world a thought, in time and a space.
Materialism shouts, of matter's might,
No magic here, just atoms in flight.

Existentialism sighs, a lonely plea,
To find your own path, wild and free,
No grand design, just choices we make,
The meaning we find, for goodness' sake

The puzzle remains, a mystery deep,
As we search for answers, while shadows
 we keep.

The Empty Canvas

Is there a reason, a grand design?
Or just a flicker, a fleeting shine?
Nihilism whispers, "Meaningless all,"
A cosmic joke, a destined fall.

Absurdism sighs, "The world's a farce,"
Find joy in chaos, leave your own mark.
But deep inside, a yearning remains,
For connection, to ease the pain

The canvas waits, a blank domain,
To paint your story, escape the rain.
Find your own meaning, a purpose to chase,
In every moment, leave your own trace.

The River of Time

The river keeps on flowing, never stopping,
Carrying all our memories, even when we are sleeping.

Laughter from when we were youth, slowing fading around.
Right now, at this moment, it is like a gentle breeze,
A short breath, a peaceful ease.

We try to hold onto things that are gone,
While time keeps slipping away, all along.
The future calls, a soft and unknown voice,
A path we have not seen, a mysterious choice.

Will we welcome it, with arms open wide,
Or be scared of the unknown, nowhere to hide?
The river keeps flowing, forever and ever,
A journey without an end, forever and never.
And us, like leaves on the water's face,
Drifting along, at life's own pace.

Life's Journey

Young and bold, the world's a prize, Dreams take flight, beneath bridge skies. Adventure calls, a restless soul, Yearning for a distance goal.

Years unfold, a steady pace, Wisdom grows, in time and space. But shadows fall, regrets arise, For chance missed, beneath the skies.

Old age creeps, a gentle hand, Memories linger, Across the land, Peace descends, a quite grace, Acceptance that comes with time.

The Tide of Grief

At first, a wave, crashing down,

Stealing breath, leaving no sound.

Disbelief washes over, cold, and deep,

A world shattered, secrets to keep.

Anger, surges, a bitter tide,

Against the loss, nowhere to hide.

Why this pain, this cruel design?

Questions linger, unanswered, divine.

Slowly, the tide begins to recede, Memories

Surface, a comforting seed. Against the loss,

Nowhere to hide. Why this pain, this cruel design?

Questions linger, unanswered, divine.

Slowly, the tide begins to recede, Memories

Surface, a comforting seed. Acceptance dawns, a

Fragile light, Grief's heavy weights, lessens its might.

Heling whispers, a gentle breeze, Carrying love on
The summer trees. The pain remains, a tender scar,
But life moves forward, reaching for afar.

Grief's Journey

Shattered

> The world feels gray, a broken vase,
> Pieces scattered, no time to waste.
> Tears like rain, a constant pour,
> Missing laughter, forevermore.

Slowly Mending

> Days turn weeks, the pain less sharp,
> Memories linger, leaving their mark.
> A gentle hand, a listening ear,
> Whispers of hope, finally appear.

New Beginnings

> The sun breaks through, a silver of light,
> Color returns, morning feels bright.
> The vase, though cracked, holding beauty still,
> A reminder of love, against all will.

Dreams Fade

As a child, I dreamt of stars,
Reaching high, beyond the bars.
Of adventure bold and grand,
A hero in a distant land.

Now the world shows me a different face,
Responsibilities in every place.
Dreams get traded, hopes subside,
For bills to pay and life to guide.

But sometimes, late at night I see,
Glimmers of that child in me.
A whisper of the dreams I hold,
A story waiting to unfold.

The Pull

The world calls loud, a siren's song, Of parties
Bright, where I belong. But deep inside, a whisper
Pleads, "Come follow Me," my spirt needs.

The pull is strong, to fit the crowd, to chase the
Fun, shout loud and proud, but god's love waits, a
Gentle hand, A peaceful path, across the land.

I long to please, to live his way, to find a balance,
No matter what happens. To love the world, yet find my peace,
And let his love my soul release.

The Ever-Changing Me

A child sees a hero, bold and bright,
A teen seeks a tribe, bathed in fading light.
A lover finds a mirror, reflecting a shared soul,
A parent finds purpose, a story to unfold.
The years keep on flowing, a river ever wide,
The self keeps on changing, with nowhere left to
Hide.

The Many Faces of War

The soldier sees fear, the dirt, the rain,
The family weeps for loss, enduring endless pain.
The politician talks of peace, yet fuels the fire's Might,
The profiteer counts coins, in the pale moonlight.

Four Sides of the Coin

The immigrant dreams, of a future so bright,
 Leaving behind shadows and stepping into light.

The border guard watches, with a watchful eye,
Protecting the borders, where hopes and fears lie.

The local wonders, with a mix of doubt and cheer,
How this new tide will impact on your life here.

The politician speaks, of numbers and gain,
Of policies and laws, in the sun and in rain.

Warming World

The scientist warns of ice caps that melt,
Of rising seas, and a future unwell.

The politician debates, of costs and of grains,
Of jobs and power, in the changing rains.

The activist pleads, for action so bold,
To save our planet, a story untold.

The denier dismisses, with a wave of the hand,
Claims it is a hoax, across the whole land.

The victim weeps, for their home swept away,
By storms and by floods, at the close of the day.

The polluter profits, from the earth's slow demise,
Ignoring the warning, in their greedy eyes.

The G A P

The poor struggle, with hunger and cold,
 A life of hardship, a story untold.

The wealthy prosper, with fortunes amassed,
Unseeing the suffering, their lives forever passed.

The politician talks about budgets and aid,
Of programs and reforms, in the shadows they are
Made.

The social worker helps, with a gentle hand,
To lift up the fallen, across the whole land.

Wires and Waves

The creator dreams, of a world interconnected,
By wires and waves, forever directed.

The consumer clicks, on screens bright and bold,
A world at their fingertips, a story untold.

The enthusiast raves, of progress so grand,
A future of wonder, across the whole land.

The skeptic fears, of a world out hand,
Of privacy lost, and a future unplanned.

The Wheel of Time

The clock ticks on, a steady beat,
A line that stretches, long and neat.
But time can bend, a twisting vine,
A cycle born, where seasons twine.

The present blooms, a fleeting grace,
A memory ghost, a fading trace.
Yet in the flow, a rhythm lies,
The wheel of time, beneath the skies.

The Shadow's Dance

The shadow looms, a chilling breath,
A fear that grips, a grip of death.
But life is a dance, a fleeting gleam,
A fading light, a fading dream.

Acceptance comes, a quite peace,
The cycle ends, the soul finds release.
Beyond the veil a mystery lies,
A whispered hope, beneath the skies.

The Cage of Choice

We THINK we choose a grand design,
But paths are set, by fate's confine.

The chains of chance, a subtle sway,
Society's gaze, who guides our way.

A web of threads, a tangled maze,
Where freedom hides in hidden ways.
But even then, a spark remains,
A bright flicker that breaks the chains.

The Brush of Truth

The brush strokes dance, a vibrant hue,
Beauty's form, in shades anew.
Impressionist dreams, a fleeting glance,
Surrealist worlds, a strange, wild dance.

Cubist shapes, a fragmented view,
Abstract forms, where colors brew.
Each artist seeks, a truth untold,
A glimpse of life, in old stories.

The Clock Tick-Tocks

The Clock Tick-Tocks, a steady beat,
Time keeps on moving, cannot be beaten.
Moments flying, memories fade,
Childhood dreams, a distant shade.

The present's here, a fleeting grace,
A smile, a touch, a warm embrace.
The future waits, a mystery deep,
What will it bring, while we all sleep?

Time marches on, a relentless flow,
Shapin, our lives, watching us grow.
Cherish each day, a precious art,
Optional sentence- Hold time close, within your heart.

Pathway

Shock first hits, a sudden blow,
The world feels strange, a dizzy show.
Denial creeps in, hard to face,
This emptiness, this empty space.

Anger flares, a burning fire,
"Why this pain?' a soul desire.
Bargaining whispers, a desperate plea,
"If I could change, oh, what would I be?"

Sadness settles, a heavy weight,
Hope feels lost, a lonely fate.
Acceptance dawns, a fragile seed,
Memories bloom, a gentle need.

Healing comes, a slow, soft rain,
Washing away the lingering pain.
Life moves on, an unusual way,
Love remains, come what may.

Dreams Evolve

Stars ignite, a canvas vast,
Childhood dreams, a boundless cast.
Explorers bold, with spirits free,
Soaring high, on wings of glee.

Realities unfold, a different hue,
Compromises are made, ambitions anew.
Yet embers glow, of passions past,
In quiet moments, they forever last.

Evolving Faith

Seeds of doubt, a gentle breeze,
Shaking branches, rustling trees.
Yet roots remain deep and strong,
In quiet moments, where do they belong?

New blossoms bloom, in unexpected ways,
Finding solace, in life's shifting maze.
A journey shared, with hearts sincere,
Hopes' gentle light, forever near.

The Web of Life

Sunlight warms, a gentle hand,
Nourishing seeds, across the land.
Birdsong fills, the morning air,
A symphony, beyond compare.

Rivers flow, a silver thread,
Life sustains, on every bed.
Each creature plays a vital part,
In nature's dances, a beating heart.

The Evolving Self

A mirror shows, a changing face,
Childhood dreams, in this fleeting space.
Experiences shape, a unique hue,
Relationships weave; a tapestry new.

Self-discovery blooms, at every stage,
Embracing strengths, turning a new page.
Identity evolves, a flowing stream,
A journey of growth, a vibrate dream.

Grateful Heart

A sunrise paints, the morning sky,
A gentle breeze, as clouds drift by.
The laughter shared, with loved ones near,
A grateful heart dispels all fear.

For simple gifts, of every day,
A helping hand, along the way,
Finding joy, in every small thing,
A peaceful mind, contentment brings.

The Seeds of Change

Open minds, like fertile ground,
Where knowledge grows, and wisdom is found.
Education lights, a guiding star,
Breaking chains and reaching far.

Empowering voices, strong and true,
Building bridges, for a new future.
A society thrives, when minds ignite,
Education's power, shines brightly.

Faces of War

The soldier's eyes, a haunted gaze,

Reflecting shadows, of war's grim maze.

The mother weeps, for a son so young,

Life cut short, a silent song.

The politician speaks, with words so grand,

Of duty bound, and a promised land.

The profiteer smiles, as profits soar,

While families grieve, and cannons roar.

The Immigrant's Journey

A distant shore, a fading light,
Leaving loved ones, in the fading night.
Hope's compass guides, a steady hand,
Seeking refuge, in a foreign land.

New horizons, a chance to bloom,
Building a future, escaping gloom.
Challenges faced, with courage bold,
A journey shared, a story told.

A Just and Equal World

Every voice deserves to be heard,
Every right must be conferred.
Breaking a future, where all are great.

Justice for all, a guiding light,
Equality's embrace, shining ever bright.
A strong society, where all can thrive,
Social justice blooms, keeping hope alive.

Digital Natives

Old eyes see screens, a blurry haze,
A world they built on bygone days.
But teens breath digital, the air they know,
A current where their futures flow.

Born to the keyboard, the pixel's gleam,
A different landscape, a waking dream.
Not just distraction, a tool so vast,
Connections forged, that forever last.

Shift the old version, the weary sigh,
See curious minds that learn and try.
Tech-savvy teens, with skills untold,
A future they are shaping, brave and bold.

The Long Goodbye

The clock ticks s l o w, a heavy beat,
Death's coming close, a bitter treat.
A scary thought, the end we fear,
Of nothing left, no one held dear.

The world fades out, a silent hush,
No more to feel, no gentle touch.
A dark unknown, a final sleep,
Secrets the grave will always keep.

We cling to life, with all our might,
Afraid to lose the sun's warm light.
The long goodbye a painful sting,
A silent song, the raven sings,

Sunset's Peace

The day is done, the light grows dim,
A quite peace, from deep within.
Life's journey ends, a natural flow,
Like gentle streams, where rivers go.

No need for tears, no fear to hold,
Just memories shared; stories told.
A time to rest, a time to be,
At one with all, eternally.

The sun goes down, a golden ray,
A promise whispered, of a new day.
A peaceful end, a gentle grace,
Finding our place, in time and space.

Painted Perfection

Glossy pages, airbrushed skin,

A perfect smile, from deep within.

The beauty ideal is so thin and bright,

A flawless image, day, and night.

Perfect poses, designer clothes,

A fantasy world, where beauty grows.

A dream of glamour, a life so grand,

Held in the pages, close at hand.

A pretty picture, a subtle lie,

A false perfection, passing by.

A painted dream, a fleeting grace,

A hollow image, In its place.

Real Beauty

Wrinkles and smiles, a story told,

A life well-lived, brave, and bold.

Real women shine, in every size,

With strength and spirit, in their eyes.

No need for filters, or perfect light,

True beauty glows, both dark and bright.

A celebration, of all we are,

Scares and laughter, near and far.

Embrace the flaws, the unique design,

A tapestry woven, truly divine.

Real beauty whispers, " you are enough,"

In every heart, gentle and tough.

Shadows and light

A darkened room, a single light,
A story told, in day and night.
The camera moves, a silent guide,
Showing us truths, that often hide.

A close-up face, a whispered word,
Emotions fell but rarely heard.
A shifting angle, a change of view,
Making us wonder what is true.

The filmmaker's art, magic spell,
Changing our thoughts, we cannot quite tell.
A story unfolds, in shades of gently play.

Twisted Tales

A simple scene, a happy day,
Can turn to darkness, in a way.
The music changes, soft and low,
A sense of dread begins to grow.

The editing cuts, fast and sharp,
Creating tension, in the dark.
A different lens, a new perspective,
The story twists were apprehensive.

What seemed so clear, Is now unclear,
The filmmaker's power is always near.
Changing our minds, with every frame,
 A cinematic, twisting game.

The **Boil**

My chest gets tight,
Head starts to pound,
Worlds are all hot,
Wanting out now.

Blood runs fast,
Breath comes hard,
Like a storm,
About to break.

Mirror, Mirror

Red face in the glass,

My eyes are flashing hot.

What makes me so mad?

I don't know what.

Is that really me?

So, mean and so loud?

I want to be calm,

Not part of the crowd.

Bottled Up

Words unsaid, a heavy heart,
A burning fire, tearing apart.
A smile I wear, a mask I hold,
But inside, a story untold.

The anger simmers, a silent storm,
My soul is bruised, my spirit warm.
I swallow the words, I bite my tongue,
But the pain lingers, where it belongs.

A hollow ache, a constant fight,
To keep the darkness from the light.
But how long can I hold it in?
Before the dam breaks, the flood begins.

The Grudge

My mind's a stage, a harsh spotlight,
Where every flaw takes center place.
I judge myself with all my might,
No room for love, no hint of grace.

This inner voice, it stings and bites,
A constant hum of "not enough."
It fills my heart with angry fights,
And piles up pain, so hard, so rough.

Resentment grows, a bitter seed,
As I compare my worst to all the rest.
Trapped in this cycle, I can't be freed,
Until I learn to give myself a rest.

Shadows Within

A dark part of me,
Hides deep inside,
It makes me angry,
And hurts my pride.

I need to see it,
Ans know it's there,
So, I can calm down,
And truly care.

Simmering

A tiny seed of rage,
Plated deep inside.
Covered up with smiles,
Nowhere left to hide.

Days turn into weeks,
Years begin to crawl.
Seedling starts to sprout,
Breaking through the wall.

Cracks appear at first,
Then a mighty roar.
Anger long suppressed,
Can't be hidden anymore.

The Art of Forgiveness

A heavy heart, a troubled mind,

Seeking peace, a way to find.

Forgiving others, a tough road,

Letting go of anger's load.

Forgiving self, a harder quest,

Accepting flaws and finding rest.

A gentle touch, a quite plea,

The art of forgiveness, setting us free.

The ~~Sting~~

A bitter taste upon my tongue,
A heavy heart, a silent song.
I see the wrong, the twisted game,
Where fairness fades, and shadows claim.

A whispered word, a hidden deed,
  A planted seed of bitter creed.
I watch it grow, a thorny vine,
And feels the sting, it cuts like brine.

My voice is small, my hands are tied,
But in my soul, a fire hides.
I'll fan the flames, and make them bright,
And fight for truth, and fight for right.

Red

Hot words fly, a burning sting,
Hurt feelings, a broken thing.
Sharp replies, a bitter tase,
Love turns into hate, a love misplaced.

The fire grows, it won't let go,
More angry words, a painful show.
A hurt so deep, it starts again,
The cycle of rage, it never ends.

Silent Walls

A word unsaid, a look away,
A coldness grows with each new day.
No angry shouts, no slamming doors,
Just quietness that cuts to the core.

A hidden hurt, a message sent,
A wall goes up, our time is spent
In chilly space, where words wont' fly.
Just silent treatment passing by.

Words That Wound

A shout, a cry, a word in haste,

A flash of anger, love misplaced.

The hurt it brings, a lasting sting,

A tender heart, no longer sings.

The words hang heavy in the air,

A fragile bond, now hard to bear.

Forgive, forget, we try our best,

But wounded spirits needs their rest.

Empty Words

A promise made, then cast side,

Like whispers lost on the ocean tide.

A hollow ache, where trust once grew,

Now anger burns, a flame so true.

Walls

A word, a look, a whispered sound,
A wall goes up, on angry, ground.
We build it high, meant to last.

But in that space, so cold and bare,
Love's gentle whispers cannot fare.
The wall stands strong, a lonely keep,
While sorrow makes the soft heart weep.

Words like Daggers

Sticks and stones may break my bones,
But words can cut and leave me prone.
Anger's fire, a burning brand,
Scares the heart and shakes the hand.

Simple words, so sharp and keen,
Can wound more deeply than ever seen.
A whispered name, a shouted slight,
Darkens the day and steals the light.

Sticks and Stones

Angry words, like stones we throw,
Leave marks that don't easily go.
A hurt inside, a silent tear,
A heavy heart, filled with fear.

We fight and shout, then walk away,
But feelings linger, day by day.
A broken trust, a painful sting,
The echo of a fight still rings.

Quiet Fury

A silent look, a turned away,
A simple thing left unsaid today.
But little hurts begin to grow,
A hidden anger, soft and low.

Each small slight, a tiny seed,
Of bitter feelings, a growing weed.
Unspoken words, a heavy weight,
Pushing love toward a closed gate.

Broken Pieces

The storm has passed, the air is still,
But broken pieces lie around.
A quiet house, a missing thrill,
Where laughter used to resound.

A pain so deep, a tear unshed,
A family torn; a love grown cold.
The angry words, the things we said,
A story sadly to be told.

Enough is Enough

A rumble starts, a quiet stir,
Then voices rise, a growing blur.
"We've had enough," they start to say,
"Things must change; there's a better way"

From hurt and pain, a fire grows,
Anger fuels where justice goes.
They march and shout, their spirit high,
For a world where all can fly.

Heavy Chains

A heavy weight, we didn't choose,
A world unfair, we can't refuse
To feel the anger, hot and deep,
While others comfort, they do keep.

The rules are bent, the games are rigged,
Our voices hushed; our spirits twigged.
But anger grows, a burning fire,
For justice sought and change desired.

Turning Away

Someone cries, a hand in need,
 but we look down, and don't take heed.
A wrong is done, plain to see,
 Yet we stay quiet, "Not me."

Our eyes are closed, our hearts are still,
As shadows grow, darkness fills.
We choose to look the other way,
And let the hurt continue on, each day.

Simple Joys

A little hum, soft and low,
Peace inside, watch good things grow.
Small things make my heart feel light,
Happy and calm, everything's right.

Warm Embrace

Sun on skin, a golden hue,
Gentle breeze, so soft and new.
Earth beneath my feet so brave,
Nature's beauty everywhere.

Birdsong sweet, a gentle sound,
Flowers blooming all around.
Scent of grass, so fresh and clean,
Joyful moments, yet unseen.

Close my eyes, and fell the light,
Nature's touch, so pure and bright.
Simple things, a happy day,
Sun-kissed Skin, along the way.

Little Eyes

Small hands reach, so quick and free,
Exploring all the world can be.
Bright eyes wide, a joyful gleam,
Discovering wonders, like a dream.

Grass so green, and the sky is so blue,
Everything's exciting, fresh, and new.
A tiny bug, a fluffy cloud,
Joyful laughter, shouted loud.

No worries then, no cares to keep,
Just happy moments, oh so deep.
A child's heart, so pure and light,
Making everything feel just right.

Small Joys

A tiny spark, a sudden gleam,
A happy thought, a waking dream.
A friendly face, a kind word said,
A little joy, though quickly fled.

A sunbeam bright, a gentle breeze,
A robin singing in the trees.
A simple thing, a moment small,
A happy feeling, holding all.

These fleeting joys, they come and go,
 But in our hearts, a warmth the sow.
So let us see, and let us find,
The little joys of every kind.

Heart's Dance

My heart beats strong, a happy drum,
Alive and here, my feelings come.
The world around, so bright and clear,
Joy at this moment, now so near.

I breathe it in, this precious air,
No time for worry, no despair.
Just feeling life, so fresh and new,
My heart's own dance, forever true.

Two Hearts as One

A knowing glance, a gentle touch,
Two souls entwined; we love so much.
We understand, no need for words,
Our hearts connect, like singing birds.

A shared smile, a knowing look,
A bond so strong, it cannot brook.
Through laughter bright and tears we've known,
Our love has steadily grown.

In quiet moments, hand in hand,
We walk together, understand.
A deep connection, pure and true,
My heart finds joy, because of you.

Happy Times

A silly joke, a funny face,
Laughter shared in any place.
With friends and family, close and near,
Joyful moments, year by year.

A gentle tease, a playful grin,
Happy sounds from deep within.
Light and fun, a happy day,
Chasing worries far away.

Together now, we laugh and play,
Making memories along the way.
Simple times, a happy band,
Joy and laughter, hand in hand.

Warm Hug

A warm hug tight, a gentle squeeze,
Safe and loved, put mind at ease.
Close together, hearts so near,
Joy in this touch, no doubt, no fear.

Friends Together

Laughing eyes and open hearts,
Sharing stories, playing parts.
Kindred spirits, side by side,
Joy and friendship, our true guide.

Through sunny days and cloudy skies,
Our bond grows strong, never dies.
Together we explore and dream,
A happy, loving, friendly team.

Giving's Gift

A happy face, a helping hand,
Joy, I give across the land.
Their smiles so bright, a warmth I feel,
My own heart mends, the wounds they heal.

But sometimes, deep inside I know,
A lonely ache begins to grow.
Their joy I share, it's true and real,
Yet something's missing, i still feel.

I give and give, my heart so free,
But where is joy just meant for me?
A quite wish, a silent plea,
To find my own true happy key.

New Day's Song

Soft light creeps, the world awakes,
A brand-new day, the sunbeam breaks.
Birds begin their happy tune,
Chasing shadows, very soon.

Fresh air blows, a gentle kiss,
The world renewed, pure bliss
Hope is born with morning light,
Everything feels good and right.

Starry Sky

Tiny lights, so far away,
Shining bright, where stars all play.
Big, wide sky, so dark and deep,
Makes me wonder, while I sleep.

Lots of stars, a pretty sight,
Sparkling gems, in dark of night.
Makes me happy, makes me dream,
Of distant worlds, it would all seem.

Life's Gentle Flow

Seeds grow tall.
Flowers bloom.
Little birds leave their cozy nest,
Nature's rhythm, truly blessed.

Sun goes up.
Sun goes down.
Life keeps moving all around.
Everything has its own time,
A happy flower, a gentle rhyme.

Creative Spark

Colors bright, a happy scene,
Pictures drawn, so fresh and keen.
Clay takes shape, has a funny face,
Building blocks in any space.

Stories told, of dragons bold,
Adventures new, and tales of old.
Singing songs, with joyful sounds,
Making art all around.

Tiny Lights

Tears may fall, and hearts may ache,
But little lights, small joy awake.
A gentle hand, a loving face,
A warm embrace, in this hard place.

Though shadows hides the sun's bright ray,
Hope still shines, along the way.
Small smiles bloom, through misty rain,
Joyful in sorrow, helps us regain.

Surprise of Joy

A simple walk, a cloudy day,
Then sunshine peeks, along the way.
A whispered word, a friendly smile,
A happy thought, that last awhile.

A quiet moment, all alone,
Then music plays, a joyful tone.
A simple gift, a kind small deed,
A planted hope, growing seed.

We look for joy in grand display,
But often find it hides away,
In little things, we didn't see,
Unexpected joy, sets our hearts free.

Why?

Why don't you get me?
Why can't you see?
Why do you laugh
When I'm in half?

Why the cold stare?
Why don't you care?
Why the quick "no"?
Why don't you know?

Why can't you hear?
Why is it unclear?
Why this hard wall?
Why don't you catch my fall?

What Is It Worth?

A simple book, a kind man's way,
"Don't forget to smell the flowers," he'd say.
No big name, but roses bright,
Quiet strength, a gentle light.

A stack of paper, words inside,
What is it worth, this whispered tide?
Like Winston's grace, so soft and low,
The worth is found in things that grow.

"Don't forget to smell the flowers," Sweet and clear,
A fragrant moment, holding dear.
In the graveyard's space, where shadows creep,
"Don't forget to smell the flowers," secrets keep.

He taught me more than just the facts,
Helped me find my own right tracks.
So, thank you, Mr. Turner.

ABOUT THE AUTHOR

Makayla is a teen writer. With three years of writing experience, she developed a passion for crafting compelling stories and evocative poetry. She is also certified in numerous things including creative writing. When she's not writing, you can find her baking or resting.

To my readers, thank you. This story is for you. Your support and imagination brings these words to life. I hope u enjoy life's journey.

Made in the USA
Columbia, SC
09 April 2025